D1114188

PENGUIN BOOKS

MARY TUDOR

Anna Whitelock is a historian of early modern Britain and the author of *The Queen's Bed: An Intimate History of Elizabeth's Court*, winner of the PEN/Jacqueline Bograd Weld Award for Biography. She teaches at Royal Holloway College, University of London, and is the director of the London Centre for Public History. A frequent television presenter and media commentator on the Tudors, the monarchy, and royal succession, she has written for the *Guardian*, the *Times Literary Supplement*, and *BBC History*.

Mary Tudor

PRINCESS, BASTARD, QUEEN

Anna Whitelock

PENGUIN BOOKS

PENGUIN BOOKS
An imprint of Penguin Random House LLC
375 Hudson Street
New York, New York 10014
penguin.com

First published in Great Britain by Bloomsbury Publishing Plc 2009
First published in the United States of America by Random House,
an imprint of The Random House Publishing Group,
a division of Random House, Inc., 2010
Published in Penguin Books 2016

Published by arrangement with Random House,
a division of Penguin Random House LLC.

Pages 401–402 constitute an extension of this copyright page.

LIBRARY OF CONGRESS CATALOGING-IN-PUBLICATION DATA

Names: Whitelock, Anna, author.
Title: Mary Tudor / Anna Whitelock.
Description: New York, New York : Penguin Books, 2016. | Includes
bibliographical references and index.
Identifiers: LCCN 2015040862 | ISBN 9780143128656
Subjects: LCSH: Mary I, Queen of England, 1516–1558. | Queens—Great
Britain—Biography. | Great Britain—History—Mary I, 1553–1558. | Great
Britain—Kings and rulers—Biography.
Classification: LCC DA347 .W48 2016 | DDC 942.05/4092—dc23

Printed in the United States of America
10 9 8 7 6 5 4 3 2 1

Set in Fournier MT Std

For Sam, Lily, and Baillie

SHE WAS A KING'S DAUGHTER,

SHE WAS A KING'S SISTER,

SHE WAS A KING'S WIFE.

SHE WAS A QUEEN,

AND BY THE SAME TITLE A KING ALSO.

—John White, bishop of Winchester,
in his sermon at Mary's funeral

CONTENTS

PART TWO · A KING'S SISTER

PART THREE · A QUEEN

PART FOUR · A KING'S WIFE

MARY TUDOR'S FAMILY TREE

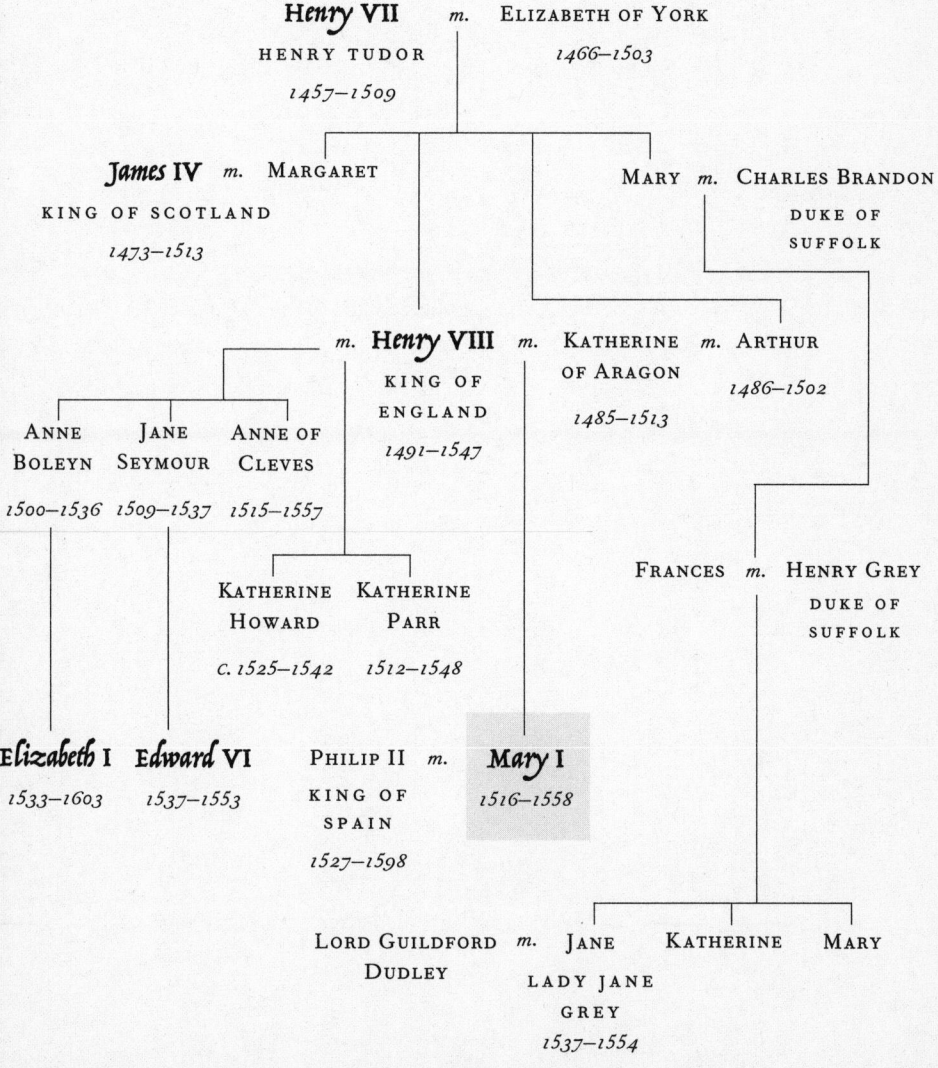

Henry VII *m.* ELIZABETH OF YORK
HENRY TUDOR   1466–1503
1457–1509

James IV *m.* MARGARET   MARY *m.* CHARLES BRANDON
KING OF SCOTLAND   DUKE OF
1473–1513   SUFFOLK

m. Henry VIII *m.* KATHERINE *m.* ARTHUR
KING OF   OF ARAGON   1486–1502
ENGLAND   1485–1513
1491–1547

ANNE   JANE   ANNE OF
BOLEYN   SEYMOUR   CLEVES
1500–1536 1509–1537 1515–1557

KATHERINE KATHERINE   FRANCES *m.* HENRY GREY
HOWARD   PARR   DUKE OF
C. 1525–1542 1512–1548   SUFFOLK

Elizabeth I Edward VI PHILIP II *m.* Mary I
1533–1603   1537–1553 KING OF   1516–1558
                        SPAIN
                        1527–1598

LORD GUILDFORD *m.* JANE   KATHERINE MARY
DUDLEY   LADY JANE
                   GREY
                   1537–1554

AUTHOR'S NOTE

∴

ARY'S REIGN HAS LONG BEEN CONSIDERED A TERRIBLE FOOTNOTE in English history, her reputation dominated by the great Elizabethan work of propaganda, John Foxe's *Actes and Monuments,* which so graphically depicted "the horrible and bloudy time of Queene Mary." It is striking that nearly 450 years later Foxe's work continues to have a tenacious hold on the popular imagination. Recently this view found dramatic expression in Shekhar Kapur's 1998 film *Elizabeth,* which portrays the dark, brutal, and barren world of Mary in contrast to the light, liberating accession of Elizabeth. Mary is maligned as a cruel, obstinate Catholic bigot who burned heretics and married an unpopular Spanish prince. As one early biographer concluded, she had "a fatal lack of that subtle appeal that awakens popular sympathies."[1]

This book seeks to challenge such popular prejudice and acceptance of Mary as one of the most reviled women in English history; to "rebrand" her less as the "grotesque charicature" that is "Bloody Mary" and more as the groundbreaking first crowned queen of England. In the last ten years or so the gap between academic writing and popular understanding has grown ever wider, and this has spurred my desire to write. Recent scholarship has questioned twentieth-century verdicts of Mary's reign as one of "sterility" and lack of achievements and of Mary as a "profoundly conventional woman."[2] A number of important revisions can now be made to the pervasive popular view.

Mary's relationship with her mother is key, and Katherine must be understood not as a weak, rejected wife but as a strong, highly accomplished, and defiant woman who withstood the attempts of her hus-band, Henry VIII, to browbeat her into submission and was determined to defend the legitimacy of her marriage and of her daughter's birth. As one of the most prolific Tudor historians of the twentieth century argued, Mary "had ever been her mother's daughter rather than her father's, devoid of political skill, unable to compromise, set only on the wholesale reversal of a generation's history."[3] Yet Katherine of Aragon can be understood as a figure of immense courage from whom Mary could learn much. Katherine oversaw Mary's early education and highly formative upbringing, which was not a prelude to inevitable fail-ure but an apprenticeship for rule. Mary's Spanish heritage informed her queenship but in a far more positive way than is popularly acknowl-edged.

Mary's very accession was against the odds and is a too commonly overlooked achievement the scale of which is rarely acknowledged. It was, as one contemporary chronicler described, an act of "Herculean daring" that rarely finds its way into the popular annals. Upon becom-ing queen, Mary entered a man's world and had to change the nature of politics—her decisions as to how she would rule would become precedents for the future. She gained the throne, maintained her rule, preserved the line of Tudor succession, and set many important prece-dents for her sister, Elizabeth. Less a victim of the men around her but politically accomplished and at the center of politics, Mary was a woman who in many ways was able to overcome the handicap of her sex. For good or ill, Mary proved to be very much her own woman and a not entirely unsuccessful one at that.

So the Mary of this book is an unfamiliar queen, and hers is an incredibly thrilling and inspirational story. She broke tradition, she challenged precedent; she was a political pioneer who redefined the English monarchy.

RESURRECTION

∴

In WESTMINSTER ABBEY, AMID THE CHAOTIC GRANDEUR OF ROYAL tombs, lies the marble effigy of a resplendent Tudor queen. It is a striking, iconic image of Elizabeth I, her successes inscribed for "eternal memory" in panegyric Latin verses. Each week hundreds of people file through the north aisle of the Chapel of Henry VII, past this monument dedicated to the great "Gloriana." Many perhaps fail to notice the Latin inscription on the base of this towering edifice:

> *Regno consortes et urna, hic obdormimus Elizabetha et Maria sorores,*
> *in spe resurrectionis.* [Partners both in throne and grave, here rest
> we two sisters, Elizabeth and Mary, in the hope of one resurrection.]

Elizabeth does not lie alone; she inhabits her elder sister's tomb.

Queen Mary I was buried there on December 14, 1558, with only stones from demolished altars marking the spot where she was laid to rest. When Elizabeth died in 1603, her body was placed in the central vault of the chapel alongside the remains of her grandparents Henry VII and Elizabeth of York. But in 1606, James I ordered that the dead queen be moved. Forty-eight years after Mary's death, the stones were cleared from her grave, the vault was reopened, and Elizabeth's coffin was placed within. Seeking to legitimize a new dynasty and preserve his status in posterity, James wanted Elizabeth's place in Henry VII's vault for himself.[1] Having moved her body, he then commissioned a monument, celebrating the life of England's Virgin Queen, to lie upon the tomb of the two dead queens. In doing so James shaped how those queens would be remembered: Elizabeth magnificent, Mary, her body, as her memory, buried beneath. This book seeks to resurrect the remarkable story of Mary, the first queen of England.

MARY'S ACCESSION WAS against the odds. It was, in many ways, emblematic of a life of both fortune and adversity, of both royal favor and profound neglect. Mary was a truly European princess. The heir of the Tudor dynasty in England and a daughter of Spain, she grew up adored at home and feted by courts across Europe. Yet this was a prelude to great personal tragedy. When her parents, Henry VIII and Katherine of Aragon, divorced, Mary, then just seventeen years old, was reduced from a royal princess to a royal bastard. She became the "Lady Mary," spurned by her father and superseded in his affections by the infant Elizabeth. For the next three years she defended her mother's honor, refusing to acknowledge her stepmother, Anne Boleyn, as queen or the illegitimacy of her own birth. Mother and daughter were prevented from seeing each other even when Katherine was dying. Mary was threatened with death as a traitor and forced to submit to her father's authority as supreme head of the English Church. Her submission defined her. From then on she lived according to the dictates of her Catholic conscience, ready to defend her faith at all costs.

Her defiance cast her in opposition to the brother she loved when he became king. Edward VI was determined to enforce a new religious service and outlaw the Mass that Mary held so dear. In repeated confrontations, Edward challenged Mary to submit to his authority, but she proved defiant, even considering flight to the imperial court in Brussels to retain her independence. As Mary refused to capitulate and accept the new Protestant settlement, Edward overturned his father's will to prevent his sister from inheriting the throne. When Edward died, the Protestant Lady Jane Grey was proclaimed queen—though she would never be crowned and anointed—and orders were issued for Mary's arrest. Yet Mary fled and eluded capture. Ready to fight for her throne, she mobilized support across East Anglia. In a dramatic coup in the summer of 1553, she mustered her forces at Framlingham Castle in Suffolk and won her rightful throne.

England had never before had a crowned queen regnant. The accession of Matilda, the daughter of Henry I, in the twelfth century had been challenged by her cousin Stephen and failed. Matilda was never crowned queen of England and granted only the title "Lady of the English."[2] It was not until Edward VI's death four hundred years later, in 1553, that England once again faced the prospect of female succession. Though there was no Salic law barring a woman from the throne, in practice the idea of female sovereignty was anathema to contemporary notions of royal majesty. The monarch was understood to be God's representative on Earth and a figure of defense and justice. Women were considered to be too weak to rule and overly led by their emotions.

Yet Mary reigned with the full measure of royal majesty; she preserved her throne against rebellion and reestablished England as a Catholic nation.

MARY'S LIFETIME SPANNED years of great European crisis, fueled by a rivalry between Spain and France. Spain had been unified in 1479 as a result of the marriage of Mary's grandparents Ferdinand of Aragon and Isabella of Castile. France had grown in strength since defeating England in the Hundred Years' War (1377–1453) and expelling the English from all its territories except Calais. In 1494, Charles VIII, the king of France, invaded Italy looking to make good his right to the Kingdom of Naples. The rival claims of France and Spain to territories in Italy ignited a conflict that would continue throughout the first half of the sixteenth century. England was now dwarfed as a European power but sought as an ally by each to prevent the ascendancy of the other. The accession of Charles of Habsburg, duke of Burgundy, as king of Spain in 1516 and as Holy Roman Emperor three years later increased the enmity with France. Mary's cousin Charles became ruler of much of central and western Europe; France was virtually encircled by Habsburg lands and challenged the emperor's claims to the disputed territories in Italy and to lands along the Pyrenees. From the eve of Mary's birth to shortly after her death, the Habsburg and Valois kings would be engaged in bitter conflict. For much of her life Mary would represent the prize of an English alliance.

Mary was born on the eve of another great struggle that divided Europe, the Reformation. In October 1517, Martin Luther ignited a battle of faith that shattered the unity of Christendom. His attack on the abuses of the Church, expressed initially in his Ninety-Five Theses, became an onslaught against many of its most fundamental teachings. Luther maintained that a sinner was justified by faith alone and salvation might not be secured by the purchase of indulgences or by other "good works." He denied the authority of the pope in Rome and called on the German princes to take over and reform the Church. With the development of printing, Luther's ideas spread, as people looked to throw off the yoke of Roman Catholicism and embrace the new teaching.

The vast empire of Charles V, Mary's cousin, became riven by rebellion and dissent. As the emperor sought to stanch the flow of Protestantism, he faced the great threat of the Ottoman Turks in the East. Under the leadership of Suleiman the Magnificent, the Turks threatened Spain's trade in the Mediterranean and Habsburg family lands in Austria. Following the fall of Constantinople in 1453, the Turkish advance had been unrelenting; Belgrade was captured and the Kingdom of Hungary conquered. From North African bases the Barbary pirates preyed on shipping and raided the coasts of Spain and Italy. During the sixteenth century, "the threat of Islam" cast a long shadow over Christian Europe, rousing successive popes to make calls for a European crusade and commanding much of the emperor's attention and resources. Throughout her life, Mary would petition Charles to come to her aid and protect her claim to the throne and later her right to practice her religion; but always she would be secondary to his own strategic interests.

England too became the theater of European conflict. Henry VIII's repudiation of Katherine of Aragon and search for a divorce challenged the power of the papacy and of Katherine's nephew Emperor Charles V. Charles was determined to protect the position of his aunt, and for a time Henry's rejection of Katherine and their daughter, Mary, brought the threat of war with Spain and the papacy. Mary would always look to her Habsburg cousin for protection. Her kinship with him gave the struggles of her life a European dimension. Remaining loyal to her Spanish ancestry and looking to preserve England's position in Europe, she chose to marry Philip, the son of the emperor and the future king of Spain. It was a match that revived the Anglo-Spanish alliance founded with her parents' marriage forty-five years before. While protecting her sovereignty as queen and limiting his power, Mary would submit to Philip as a dutiful wife and mourn his long absences abroad.

It is the contrast between Mary as queen and the personal tragedy of Mary as a woman that is the key to understanding her life and reign. Her private traumas of phantom pregnancies, debilitating illnesses, and rejection—first by her father and then by her husband—were played out in the public glare of the fickle Tudor court. The woman who emerges is a complex figure of immense courage and resolve, her dramatic life unfolding in the shadow of the great sixteenth-century struggle for power in Europe.

MARY TUDOR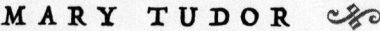

PART ONE

A King's Daughter

CHAPTER I

PRINCESS OF ENGLAND

⸫

MARY, THE DAUGHTER OF KING HENRY VIII AND KATHERINE OF Aragon, was born at four in the morning of Monday, February 18, 1516, at Placentia, the royal palace at Greenwich, on the banks of the Thames River in London. Three days later, the nobility of England gathered at the royal apartments to form a guard of honor as the baby emerged from the queen's chamber in the arms of Katherine's devoted friend and lady-in-waiting, Elizabeth Howard, countess of Surrey. Beneath a gold canopy held aloft by four knights of the realm, the infant was carried to the nearby Church of the Observant Friars.[1] It was the day of Mary's baptism, her first rite of passage as a royal princess.

The procession of gentlemen, ladies, earls, and bishops paused at the door of the church, where, in a small arras-covered wooden archway, Mary was greeted by her godparents, blessed, and named after her aunt, Henry's favorite sister. The parade then filed two by two into the church, which had been specially adorned for the occasion. Jewel-encrusted needlework hung from the walls; a font, brought from the priory of Christchurch Canterbury and used only for royal christenings, had been set on a raised and carpeted octagonal stage, with the accoutrements for the christening—basin, tapers, salt, and chrism—laid out on the high altar.[2] After prayers were said and promises made, Mary was plunged three times into the font water, anointed with the holy oil, dried, and swaddled in her baptismal robe. As Te Deums were sung, she was taken up to the high altar and confirmed under the sponsorship of Margaret Pole, countess of Salisbury.[3] Finally, with the rites concluded, her title was proclaimed to the sound of the heralds' trumpets:

> God send and give long life and long unto the right high, right noble and excellent Princess Mary, Princess of England and daughter of our most dread sovereign lord the King's Highness.[4]

Despite the magnificent ceremony, the celebrations were muted. This was not the longed-for male heir, but a girl.

SIX YEARS EARLIER, in the Church of the Observant Friars, Henry had married his Spanish bride, Katherine of Aragon. Within weeks of the wedding, Katherine was pregnant and Henry wrote joyfully to his father-in-law, Ferdinand of Aragon, proclaiming the news: "Your daughter, her Serene Highness the Queen, our dearest consort, has conceived in her womb a living child and is right heavy therewith."[5] Three months later, as England awaited the birth of its heir, Katherine miscarried. Yet the news was not made public, and with her belly still swollen, most likely with an infection, she was persuaded by her physician that she "remained pregnant of another child."[6] A warrant was issued for the refurbishment of the royal nursery, and in March 1511 she withdrew to her apartments in advance of the birth.[7]

For weeks the court waited for news of the delivery, but labor did not come. As Katherine's confessor, Fray Diego, reported, "it has pleased our Lord to be her physician in such a way that the swelling decreased."[8] There was no baby. Luiz Caroz, the new Spanish ambassador, angrily condemned those who had maintained "that a menstruating woman was pregnant" and had made her "withdraw publicly for her delivery."[9] Many councillors now feared that the queen was "incapable of conceiving."[10] Fearing her father's displeasure, Katherine wrote to Ferdinand in late May, four months after the event, claiming that only "some days before" she had miscarried a daughter and failing to mention the subsequent false pregnancy. Do "not be angry," she begged him, "for it has been the will of God."[11]

Hope soon revived, and while writing letters of deceit to her father, Katherine discovered she was pregnant once more.[12] Seven months later, on the morning of New Year's Day, bells rang out the news of the safe delivery of a royal baby. It was a living child and a son; England had its male heir. Celebrations engulfed the court and country, and five days later the child was christened and proclaimed "Prince Henry, first son of our sovereign lord, King Henry VIII." The king rode to the Shrine of Our Lady at Walsingham in Norfolk to give thanks and hold a splendid joust in his son's honor. But the celebrations were short-lived. Three weeks later Prince Henry died. It did not augur well. Over the next seven years, failed pregnancy followed failed pregnancy, each ending in miscarriage, stillbirth, or infant death.

So when in the spring of 1515 the thirty-one-year-old queen fell pregnant for the seventh time, there was a somewhat subdued response. This pregnancy, however, followed its natural course, and in the early weeks of the New Year the royal couple moved to the royal palace at Greenwich, where Henry had been born twenty-four years before and where preparations were now under way for the queen's confinement.

The Royal Book, the fifteenth-century book of court etiquette for all such royal events drawn up by Margaret Beaufort, Henry VIII's grand-mother, outlined the necessary arrangements. The queen's chamber was to be turned into a tapestried cocoon, the floor covered with thickly laid carpet; the walls, ceiling, and windows hung with rich arras and one window left loosely covered to allow in air and light. The wall tapes-tries, the queen's canopied bed, and the bed hangings were to be of sim-ple design, with figurative images avoided for fear of provoking dreams that might disturb mother and child. There was to be a cupboard stacked with gold and silver plate to signify the queen's status, and crucifixes, candlesticks, images, and relics placed on an altar before which she could pray. At the foot of her canopied bed was placed a daybed, cov-ered with a quilt of crimson satin and embroidered with the king and queen's arms, where the birth would take place.[13]

In late January, with all made ready, Katherine began the ceremony of "taking her chamber." First she went to the Chapel Royal to hear Mass; then, returning to the Presence Chamber, she sat beneath her cloth of estate—the mark of her rank—and took wines and spices with members of the court. Lord Mountjoy, her chamberlain, called on everyone to pray that "God would give her the good hour"—safe delivery—and the queen was accompanied to the door of her bedchamber in solemn procession. There the men departed, and Katherine entered the exclusively female world of childbirth. As *The Royal Book* stipulated, "All the ladies and gentlewomen to go in with her, and no man after to come in to the chamber save women, and women to be inside."[14] She would not be in male company again until her "churching," the purification after labor, thirty days after the birth. Officers, butlers, and other servants would bring all manner of things to the chamber door, but there the women would receive them.

After days of seclusion and hushed expectancy, the February dawn was broken with bells ringing in the news: the queen had delivered a healthy baby, but a girl. Writing two days later, Sebastian Giustiniani, the Venetian ambassador, assured the doge and Senate that he would offer their congratulations but added that, had the baby been a son, "[he] should have already done so, as in that case, it would not have been fit to delay the compliment."[15] Eventually, the ambassador sought an audience with King Henry and congratulated him "on the birth of his daughter, and on the wellbeing of her most serene mother Queen." The state would have been "yet more pleased," he added, "had the child been a son." Henry remained optimistic. "We are both young," he insisted; "if it was a daughter this time, by the grace of God, sons will follow."[16]

CHAPTER 2

A TRUE FRIENDSHIP AND ALLIANCE

∴

We have this moment received news of the death of the most serene Ferdinand, King of Aragon; and it is supposed this was known some days ago to his Majesty, but kept secret, because of the most serene Queen's being on the eve of her delivery.[1]

—GIUSTINIANI TO THE DOGE
AND SENATE, FEBRUARY 20, 1516

MARY CAME INTO THE WORLD DURING A SEASON OF MOURNING. Just days before her birth, news reached the English court of the death of Katherine's father. Solemn requiems were sung at St. Paul's, but the queen was not informed of her loss until after she had safely given birth.[2] Ferdinand's death marked the passing of the last of Mary's grandparents, and though she never knew any of them, with her steely determination, Catholic devotion, and strong sense of her right to rule, she would prove to be every inch their heir. She was, unmistakably, both a Spaniard and a Tudor.

Her mother, Katherine, was the daughter of Ferdinand of Aragon and Isabella of Castile, her father the son of Henry Tudor (Henry VII) and Elizabeth of York. Both sets of grandparents had brought unity to their war-torn kingdoms after years of disputed successions. Henry Tudor's defeat of Richard III at the Battle of Bosworth in 1485 had ended thirty-three years of incipient civil war between the Houses of York and Lancaster, two rival branches of the Plantagenet family that had ruled England since the twelfth century. Henry, a Lancastrian, claimed the throne through his mother, Margaret Beaufort, and her descent from John of Gaunt, duke of Lancaster, the son of Edward III.

Following the accession of the Yorkist king, Edward IV, in 1471, Henry had fled to Brittany for fear that Edward would act against him as the remaining Lancastrian claimant. Twelve years later, after Edward had died, his brother Richard, duke of Gloucester, usurped the throne. He imprisoned, and most likely murdered, his nephew Edward V, and was crowned King Richard III on July 6, 1483. Realizing Richard's unpopularity, Henry saw an opportunity to win the throne. He set sail from Brittany with French men and ships and landed at Milford Haven in August 1485. On the twenty-second he overwhelmed the king's forces at Bosworth, near Leicester, and killed Richard III in the midst of the battle. Five months after his accession, Henry married Elizabeth of York, the eldest daughter and surviving heir of the Yorkist king, Edward IV, thereby uniting the warring Plantagenet family. The establishment of the Tudor dynasty was made secure by the birth of their first son and heir, Arthur, on September 19, 1486, a daughter Margaret, and a second son, Prince Henry, five years later, to be followed by another daughter, Mary.

Mary's grandmother Isabella of Castile had also fought to win her throne, after her father disinherited her. Alongside her husband Ferdinand, king of Aragon, she campaigned for five years in a bitter civil war before emerging triumphant and claiming the crown of Castile. The only queen regnant in fifteenth-century Europe, she doggedly reasserted her position in the face of her husband's attempts to share her power. It would be a marriage of equals, with both sovereigns ruling in their own right. Ferdinand and Isabella became the foremost monarchs in Europe, with a crusading zeal that characterized the Spanish monarchy. Their shared aim became the Reconquista of Granada, the last Muslim kingdom in Spain. The Reconquista was to be the climax of the Crusade, the medieval Christian enterprise against the Muslims that had begun in the twelfth century. Isabella, determined, single-minded, and fervently Catholic, saw the campaign as her divine purpose and rode with her knights, rallying her troops. The war lasted for ten years before finally, on January 2, 1492, the last Muslim leader, Muhammad II, surrendered complete control of Granada. It was the culmination of several centuries of reconquest and a great Christian triumph. In the years that followed, the Spanish Inquisition, established first in Castile and then in Aragon, secured the expulsion of all remaining

Jews and Muslims. "The Catholic Kings," as they were entitled by Pope Alexander IV, had created a unified Spain and an entirely Catholic kingdom.

Katherine, the youngest of Ferdinand and Isabella's five children, was born on December 16, 1485, in the midst of the Reconquista at the archbishop of Toledo's palace northeast of Madrid. She was named after her mother's English grandmother, a daughter of John of Gaunt, duke of Lancaster, who had married Enrique III of Castile. Following the defeat of the Moors, the Alhambra—the former residence of the Muslim kings—became Katherine's home, and from there she witnessed the expulsion of the Jews and the activities of the Inquisition.

Isabella was determined that her four daughters be educated properly and have what she had been denied. She had received only a meager schooling as a child and had later taught herself to read Latin while campaigning. Along with learning the "female arts" of dancing, music, needlework, and embroidery, Katherine learned the works of the Latin Fathers of the Church—Ambrose, Augustine, Gregory, and Jerome— and those of the Latin Christian poets. But whereas her brother, Juan, was educated to rule, Katherine and her sisters were expected to cement foreign policy alliances as the wives of European princes. First Isabella, Katherine's eldest sister, was married to Prince Alfonso of Portugal, then Juana to the Archduke Philip of Burgundy, and later Maria to Prince Manoel of Portugal. When it was Katherine's turn, her parents looked to England.

Ferdinand and Isabella wanted an Anglo-Spanish alliance as a counterpoise to French aggression in Italy. For Henry VII a union with Spain was a great diplomatic coup, a means to bolster the fledgling Tudor dynasty and England's place in Europe. Founded on their common interest of restraining the growing power of France, the Treaty of Medina del Campo of March 28, 1489, provided for mutual cooperation. It would form the basis of an Anglo-Spanish bond that would endure for the first half of the sixteenth century.

A true friendship and alliance shall be observed henceforth between Ferdinand and Isabella, their heirs and subjects, on the one part, and Henry, his heirs and subjects, on the other part. They promise to assist one another in defending their present and future dominions against any enemy whatsoever. . . . As often as and whenever Ferdinand and Isabella make war with France, Henry shall do the same, and conversely. . . . In order to strengthen this alliance the Princess Katherine is to marry Prince Arthur. The marriage is to be contracted *per verba de futuro* as soon as Katherine and Arthur attain the necessary age.[3]

Isabella "made very particular honour [of the English ambassadors], for she prized her Lancastrian kinship with Henry, and saw a connection with England, as with Burgundy, important to pre-eminence in Europe."[4] And so, from the age of three, Katherine knew her future would be as an English queen. Her mother was reluctant for her to go: she was the youngest of her children and the last to marry; but finally, aged sixteen, Katherine set sail for England to marry Henry VII's son Arthur.[5] Upon the Spanish princess's arrival at Plymouth, the licentiate Alcares wrote to tell Isabella that "she could not have been received with greater rejoicings if she had been the Saviour of the World."[6]

Katherine and Arthur were married on November 14, 1501, at St. Paul's Cathedral. It was a magnificent ceremony and one that heralded the Anglo-Spanish alliance—the defining moment of the Tudor dynasty.[7] After a week of splendid banquets and tournaments, the royal couple journeyed to Ludlow in Shropshire to govern the Principality of Wales, as was the ancient custom for the heir to the throne. But though long in the making, the marriage was to last less than six months. On April 2, Arthur, then sixteen, died suddenly; most accounts suggest it was tuberculosis, or "consumption." The foundations on which the Anglo-Spanish entente had been constructed had crumbled.

Yet it was an alliance too important for either party to lose. As soon as news reached Spain of Arthur's death, Ferdinand and Isabella mooted the possibility of Katherine marrying the new heir to the throne, ten-year-old Prince Henry. Because of their consanguinity, a dispensation had to be sought from Pope Julius II, although Katherine insisted that her marriage to Arthur had never been consummated. On June 23, 1503, a new treaty was signed and agreement reached for Prince Henry and Katherine to be married in five years' time. But when Queen Isabella died in November 1504, the personal union of Castile and Aragon, founded on her marriage with Ferdinand, was shattered. Isabella had bequeathed Castile to her daughter Juana, who was married to Philip of Burgundy. He claimed the throne in her name, while Ferdinand of Aragon took power as regent. Katherine's worth as a bride fell dramatically. She was no longer princess of the Iberian Peninsula, and an alliance with Aragon alone was of limited value. Henry VII now abandoned marriage negotiations with Ferdinand.

Katherine, meanwhile, was stranded. She remained in England, mourning the loss of her mother, with little money and no clear status. She petitioned her father to come to her aid, describing how she was in debt and how greatly she needed money "not for extravagant things" but "only for food"; she was "in the greatest trouble and anguish in the world."[8]

ON APRIL 21, 1509, amid scenes of great celebration, seventeen-year-old Prince Henry was proclaimed king of England. "Heaven and earth rejoices," wrote Lord Mountjoy to the Dutch humanist Desiderius Erasmus; "everything is full of milk and honey and nectar. Avarice has fled the country. Our King is not after gold, or gems, or precious metals, but virtue, glory, immortality."[9] Soon after his accession, Henry sought to establish his European status by reasserting England's claim to the French Crown. He needed allies and looked to renew the alliance with Ferdinand of Aragon and marry his brother's widow, Katherine. On June 11 they exchanged vows at the Franciscan church at Greenwich.

"Most illustrious Prince," Henry was asked, "is it your will to fulfil the treaty of marriage concluded by your father, the late King of England and the parents of the Princess of Wales, the King and Queen of Spain; and, as the Pope has dispensed with this marriage, to take the Princess who is here present for your lawful wife?" Both parties answered, "I will."[10]

Two weeks later, Henry and Katherine were crowned together at Westminster Abbey. He was eighteen, handsome, and athletic; she was twenty-three and described as "the most beautiful creature in the world." Well educated and accomplished, she loved music, dancing, and hawking almost as much as Henry did. She was, in many ways, the ideal royal bride. Both were equally learned and pious and were keen readers of theological works. Katherine spent hours at her devotions, rising at midnight to say Matins and at dawn to hear Mass, and, very much her mother's daughter, she proved to be politically able and determined. As Henry prepared for war with France in 1512, Katherine was closely involved. "The King is for war, the Council against and the Queen for it," one Venetian diplomat reported.[11]

While Henry embarked on his campaign, capturing the towns of Thérouanne and Tournai in northern France, Katherine remained in England as "Regent and Governess of England, Wales and Ireland," with authority to raise troops and supervise preparations for war against the Scots. Ten years earlier, when James IV of Scotland had married Henry's elder sister, Margaret, he had sworn "perpetual peace" with England. He had now been persuaded by the French to renew their "auld alliance" against England. War was declared in August, and James launched an invasion across the border. As Peter Martyr, the contemporary Italian historian, reported:

> Queen Katherine, in imitation of her mother Isabella . . . made splendid oration to the English captains, told them to be ready to defend their territory . . . and they should remember that English courage excelled that of all other nations. Fired by these words, the nobles marched against the Scots . . . and defeated them.[12]

The Scottish king was killed at Flodden Field. It was one of England's most resounding victories over the Scots and Katherine's finest hour. She wrote triumphantly to Henry, "In this your grace shall see how I can keep my promise, sending you for your banners a King's coat. I thought to send himself unto you, but our Englishmen's hearts would not suffer it."[13] Following in the footsteps of her mother, Isabella, she had proved to be a great warrior queen, mustering troops and delivering rousing orations. Ironically, it would be the womanly "duties" of pregnancy and childbirth—her inability to provide a male heir—that would be her undoing.

CHAPTER 3

ARE YOU THE DAUPHIN
OF FRANCE?

∴

ONCE MARY HAD BEEN CHRISTENED, KATHERINE ENTRUSTED HER care to the staff of the royal nursery. Katherine carefully selected each of them: a lady mistress, Lady Margaret Bryan, formerly one of Katherine's ladies-in-waiting, headed the small establishment; a wet nurse, Katherine Pole, suckled the young princess; three "rockers" took it in turn to soothe her; and a laundress performed the endless task of washing the infant's clothes. In the inner room of her nursery suite, Mary slept in an "everyday" cradle. In the outer chamber, she received visitors in a specially constructed "cradle of estate," draped in a quilt of ermine and framed by a canopy embossed with the royal arms.[1] Courted by princes from around the world, she was at once dependent infant and esteemed European princess.

Her father doted on her. According to Sebastian Giustiniani, one day the king showed him the Princess Mary, then two years old, in her nurse's arms. "He drew near, knelt and kissed her hand, for that alone is kissed by any duke or noble of the land." Henry then said proudly to the envoy, *"Domine Orator, per Deum immortalem, ista puella nunquam plorat"*—this child never cries—to which Giustiniani replied, "Sacred Majesty, the reason is that her destiny does not move her to tears; she will even become Queen of France." These words pleased the king greatly.[2]

The twenty-five-year-old King Henry looked to hold his own against Francis I, the young new king of France, and Charles, duke of Burgundy, just sixteen, who had become king of Spain weeks before. Mary would increasingly become a pawn in their European rivalry.

Francis had triumphed in the latest conflict over Milan in Italy, and the warring kings had come to terms in the Treaty of Noyon. With neither side looking to England for an offensive alliance against the other, Thomas Wolsey, Henry's chief minister, sought to preserve England's status by becoming champion of peace. The Treaty of London, brokered by Wolsey in early October 1518, bound all the great powers to perpetual concord, to maintain peace and act together against any aggressor.[3] Sponsored by Pope Leo X, its declared aim was a European crusade against the Ottoman Turks, but for Henry and Wolsey it was a means of countering the growing threat of France. The treaty was underpinned by an Anglo-French rapprochement that hinged on a future marriage between Mary and the French dauphin, François, then just a few months old.[4] Although Mary was not to be delivered to France until she was sixteen and the dauphin fourteen, the betrothal sealed a new era of Anglo-French relations, which was to be celebrated the following year at a meeting of the two kings.

AT EIGHT O'CLOCK on the morning of Tuesday, October 5, 1518, Mary, just two and a half years old, was taken to her mother's chamber at Greenwich Palace in preparation for her betrothal. There her parents, the papal legates, Cardinal Wolsey and Cardinal Lorenzo Campeggio, the queen dowager of France, and numerous French dignitaries headed by the lord admiral, Guillaume Bonnivet, gathered to receive her. As Giustiniani described it, "all the court were in such rich array that I never saw the like either here or elsewhere."[5] Dressed "in cloth of gold, with a cap of black velvet on her head, adorned with many jewels," Mary was a vision of royal extravagance.[6] When Cuthbert Tunstall, the bishop of Durham, delivered his sermon in praise of marriage, she grew restless and was picked up and "taken in arms" by her lady mistress, Margaret Bryan.[7] Her betrothed, the six-month-old François, was spared the monotony of the ceremony, the lord admiral acting in his place.

After the vows were exchanged, Wolsey "placed on her finger a small ring in which a large diamond was set," leaving to Bonnivet, the proxy groom, the symbolic task of slipping it down over the second joint.[8] In spite of her young age, Mary did, it seems, know something of the meaning of the occasion. "Are you the Dauphin of France?" she was reported to have said to Bonnivet. "If you are, I wish to kiss you."[9] With the ceremony finally concluded, the party moved to the chapel for a celebratory Mass followed by a sumptuous banquet. The dancing continued long into the night, many hours after the young bride-to-be had been put to bed.

As a condition of the marriage alliance, the French had insisted that Mary be recognized as her father's heir. It was the first acknowledgment of her right to the throne.[10] At the time it seemed a relatively insignificant concession. Katherine was pregnant, and Henry held out great hope for the imminent birth of a son. But once again, to the "vexation of everyone,"[11] disappointment followed. On November 9, a month after the betrothal ceremonies, Katherine gave birth to a stillborn daughter. "Never had the kingdom desired anything so passionately as it had a prince," Giustiniani wrote. "Perhaps had the event taken place before the conclusion of the betrothal, that event might not have come to pass; the sole fear of this kingdom, that it may pass through this marriage into the power of the French."[12] By the beginning of 1519, Princess Mary, betrothed to the French dauphin, was the sole heir to the throne of England.

CHAPTER 4

A VERY FINE YOUNG
COUSIN INDEED

.·.

IN 1519, THE HABSBURG-VALOIS STRUGGLE FOR EUROPEAN DOMI-nance imploded. Mary's cousin, nineteen-year-old Charles of Spain and Burgundy, became Holy Roman Emperor following the death of his grandfather. He was now the most powerful ruler in Christendom, heir to the vast territories of Spain, Burgundy, and the Netherlands and huge swaths of Germany. England held the balance of power. Francis needed English friendship to prevent French encirclement; Charles wanted English money and ships to suppress the Comuneros revolt, which had broken out in Castile against his rule. Seeking to maximize his advantage, Henry negotiated with both sides. While rumors circulated of a proposed marriage between Mary and her cousin the Emperor Charles, Henry sought to reassure Francis of his commitment to the Anglo-French match.

On Saturday, May 26, 1520, shortly before Henry's long-awaited meeting with the French king, Charles arrived in England on his way from Spain to the Low Countries. He landed at Dover and was conducted by Henry and Wolsey to Canterbury, where for the first time he met his aunt. Katherine "embraced him tenderly, not without tears." Their reunion had been "her greatest desire in the world."[1] For three days, amid lavish entertainment, Charles sought to undermine the marriage alliance between his cousin Mary and the Valois prince. On the twenty-ninth, Henry and Katherine set sail for France accompanied by a retinue of six thousand Englishmen and -women.

For just over three weeks, a temporary town, the Camp du Drap d'Or, or Field of the Cloth of Gold, stood on a no-man's-land between the English-held town of Guisnes and French-held Ardres.[2] Gold fountains flowed with claret; there were huge and elaborate pavilions and tents and a great temporary palace of classical design erected at the town's entrance. Together the two kings jousted, feasted, and celebrated the entente reached two years before. It was a spectacular meeting of two young and physically powerful monarchs, whose rivalry was at once political and intensely personal. It was the greatest and most conspicuous display of wealth and culture that Europe had ever seen.

While her parents feasted in France, Mary became the focus of royal attention, holding court at Richmond Palace. Her nursery had been expanded to become a more "princely" household, reflecting her status—albeit reluctantly acknowledged—as the king's sole heir. Head officers were appointed, and male servants, gentlemen, grooms, and valets were added to her original female staff. Lady Bryan was replaced as lady mistress by one of the most powerful and influential women in England: Mary's godmother, Margaret Pole, the countess of Salisbury—one of Katherine's most trusted and long-serving confidantes and a direct descendant of Edward IV's brother, George, duke of Clarence. It proved to be an inspired choice. Mary became devoted to her new governess and came to think of her as a "second mother."[3]

During this time privy councillors visited the young princess frequently and sent reports to her parents in France. As one letter explained, "We have sundry times visited and seen your dearest daughter the princess, who, God be thanked, is in prosperous health and convalescence; and like as she increaseth in days and years, so doth she in grace, wit and virtue."[4] Another of June 13, 1520, described Mary as "right merry . . . and daily exercising herself in virtuous pastimes and occupations."[5]

As she was the betrothed wife of their dauphin, the French also monitored Mary's health and development. Queen Claude, Francis's wife, sent gifts of a jeweled cross "worth six thousand ducats" and a portrait of her son.[6] Anxious to see that she was fit and well after a rumor of her death, Francis sent three gentlemen to visit Mary.[7] On Saturday, June 30, the French delegation arrived by barge at Richmond and found Mary surrounded by a throng of lords, ladies, gentlemen, and gentlewomen, as befitted the heir to the throne and future queen consort of France.[8] As the envoys reported, she welcomed them "with most goodly countenance, proper communication and pleasant pastime in playing at the virginals, that they greatly marvelled and rejoiced the same, her young and tender age considered."[9] She was, of course, only four.

AFTER THE ANGLO-FRENCH entertainments were concluded, Henry rode to meet Charles V at Gravelines, Flanders, and returned with him to Calais the following day to begin negotiations. Meanwhile, Francis had taken advantage of the Comuneros revolt in Spain to reconquer Spanish Navarre. The emperor appealed to Henry for help under the Treaty of London, which had provided against such acts of aggression, and asked that he repudiate the French match and now accept him as a suitor for Mary. But Henry was keen to maintain his advantage and, though agreeing not to make any fresh treaty with the French, was reluctant to commit fully to an alliance with the emperor.

By the following year, Charles had made extravagant promises to secure an alliance, and Henry promised to declare war on France if the fighting continued until November and to mount a joint invasion within two years.[10] In these changed circumstances, Mary would be betrothed to her cousin the emperor.[11] Mary was five; Charles was twenty-one. He would have to wait eight years for Mary to be of marriageable age. As Henry acknowledged to his envoy, Cuthbert Tunstall, bishop of Durham, their agreement would "not prevent the Emperor from marrying any woman of lawful age before our daughter comes to mature years, as he will only be bound to take her if he is then at liberty." However, in order to win favorable terms from the emperor, "it is to be considered that she is now our sole heir and may succeed to the crown."[12] If Charles proved "intractable," Tunstall was instructed to warn him of what was likely to happen if the alliance was not concluded and the French marriage went ahead:

> If the match goes on between Mary and the Dauphin and he
> becomes King of France, and in her right, King of England, the
> navies of England and France will shut [the emperor] out of
> the seas. If he made his abode in Spain, the Low Countries will

be in danger, and the French King, having these two realms and the duchy of Milan, might do him great mischief in Naples and soon attain the monarchy of all Christendom. Whereas by this alliance the Emperor might get that power to himself, and put France in such perplexity as to be no longer able to trouble him.[13]

With both France and Spain seeking an English alliance, Mary was at the very center of European affairs. Katherine particularly favored the continuation of the Anglo-Spanish alliance inaugurated by her own betrothal to Prince Arthur thirty years before. When Charles Poupet de Lachaulx, the imperial ambassador, visited England in March 1522, Katherine was anxious to display her daughter's precocious abilities and would not let him leave until he had seen Mary dance. She "did not have to be asked twice" and performed with no hint of infant shyness, twirling "so prettily that no woman in the world could do better." Mary then played the virginals and "two or three songs on the spinet" with impressive accomplishment. As Lachaulx reported to Charles, "Indeed, sire, she showed unbelievable grace and skill and such self-command as a woman of twenty might envy. She is pretty and very tall for her age, just turned seven and a very fine young cousin indeed."[14]

It was exactly the response that Katherine had hoped for. Mary now chose Charles as her valentine and wore a golden brooch at her breast with "Charles" spelled out in jewels and owned another spelling out "the Emperour," which appears pinned to her bodice in a portrait miniature by Lucas Horenbout.[15] The marriage of her daughter to her nephew was a prospect that Katherine relished. As the imperial ambassador wrote to Charles, "her greatest desire, was to see you here and to receive you with the greatest honour and best cheer possible."[16]

ON MAY 26, CHARLES returned to England to celebrate the signing of the new treaty and his betrothal to Mary. He was met at Dover by Wolsey and a train of noblemen and conducted to Canterbury, where the king greeted him. Together they took the royal barge from Gravesend to Greenwich, arriving in the early evening. "At the hall door the Queen and the Princess and all the ladies received and welcomed him . . . and the Emperor had great joy to see the Queen his Aunt and especially his young cousin germain the Lady Mary."[17] Mary was again expected to perform and impress. She danced and played the virginals once more and won the praise of all those who looked on. As one envoy reported, "she promises to become a handsome lady, although it is difficult to form an idea of her beauty as she is still so small."[18]

Little over a week later, Charles was formally received into the City of London amid great pageantry. At London Bridge two giant figures of Samson and Hercules had been erected, and at Leadenhall, Italian merchants had constructed a genealogical tree showing their joint ancestry. The two monarchs then moved to Windsor, where for a month they jousted, hunted, and feasted before concluding a permanent treaty of peace and friendship that confirmed the Anglo-imperial match.[19] Charles's negotiators had at first insisted that Mary be delivered to them the following year so that she could be trained as a lady of the imperial court, but Wolsey had resisted. Mary would not go to the Habsburg court in Brussels until she was twelve, the lawful age of cohabitation, when she would become Charles's consort.[20] This fact was to dominate the next four years of her life. She was to be transformed as rapidly as possible into a Spanish lady, to be dressed "according to the fashion and manner of those parts," trained in Spanish customs and politeness, and educated in a suitable manner.[21]

CHAPTER 5

THE INSTITUTION OF A CHRISTIAN WOMAN

·.·

As concerning the bringing up of her, if he [King Henry, her father] should seek a Mistress for her to frame her after the manner of Spain, and of whom she might take example of virtue, he should not find in all Christendom a more mete than she now hath, that is to say, the Queen's grace, her mother, who is cometh of this house of Spain and who, for the affection she beareth to the Emperor, will nourish her, and bring her up as may be hereafter to his most contentment.[1]

—CUTHBERT TUNSTALL, BISHOP OF LONDON,
AND SIR RICHARD WINGFIELD, ENGLISH
AMBASSADORS TO THE EMPEROR, JULY 8, 1525

MARY WAS NOW TO BE EDUCATED AS THE FUTURE WIFE OF THE emperor and, if she remained sole heir to Henry's crown, queen of England. While it was a prospect that Henry was reluctant to accept, Katherine shared none of Henry's qualms about her daughter's right to succeed and the ability of women to govern. Her mother, Isabella, had ruled as queen of Castile and refused to yield to pressure to alter the Castilian laws that permitted her eldest daughter to succeed her. She had asserted her equality with Ferdinand in their roles as the "Catholic Kings" but had also acknowledged the importance of her role as dutiful wife and mother. For Katherine, female sovereignty was compatible with wifely obedience and there was no good reason why Mary should not succeed her father. Katherine was determined to prepare her daughter for rule.

In this she drew on her own education and experience. She consulted leading scholars and commissioned educational treatises to advise on Mary's program of instruction. Desiderius Erasmus, the great Dutch humanist, had produced the *Institutio Principis Christiani* (Institution of a Christian Prince) in 1516, but there was no similar guide for the education of a future queen regnant. Katherine requested the Spanish humanist Juan Luis Vives to write such a manual for the education of girls. As Vives wrote in his dedicatory letter of April 5, 1523, to his *De Institutione Feminae Christianae* (The Institution of a Christian Woman):

Moved by the holiness of your life and your ardent zeal for sacred studies, I have endeavoured to write something for your Majesty on the education of the Christian Woman . . . your daughter Mary will read these recommendations and will reproduce them as she models herself on the example of your goodness and wisdom to be found within your home. She will do this assuredly, and unless she alone belies all human expectations, must of necessity be virtuous and holy as the offspring of you and Henry VIII, such a noble and honoured pair.[2]

While asserting that women should be properly educated, *De Institutione* was traditional in expecting women to be men's subjugated companions; their primary goals were virtue, domesticity, and chastity. Female education, Vives maintained, was preparation not for a public role but for the conventional occupations of wife and mother. As Vives explained, men would benefit from having educated spouses, as "there is nothing so troublesome as sharing one's life with a person of no principles." Since a woman "that thinketh alone, thinketh evil," it was recommended that Mary be kept away from the company of men and be surrounded at all times with "sad, pale and untrimmed" servants.

Two lists, one of "good" books—predominantly Spanish and French—the other of *libri pestiferi*—noxious books—were recommended for Mary's reading. Chivalric romances were to be avoided, as they were thought to incite women's imaginations and corrupt their minds, given their moral frailty. Instead, Mary should read the Bible, particularly the Gospels, Acts of the Apostles, and Epistles, every morning and evening, together with the works of the Church Fathers and writers such as Plato, Cicero, and Seneca.[3] Besides reading, Vives approved of the classical female recreations of spinning, needlework, and cooking, as all such activities put off the moral danger of idleness. He concluded that Mary should follow her mother in virtue, rather than her father to the throne.

But Vives's treatise lacked detail, and in October 1524, Katherine commissioned Vives to write a more specific curriculum of study for her seven-year-old daughter. The resulting *De Ratione Studii Puerilis* (On a Plan of Study for Children) was dedicated to the young princess herself. It set out rules for the proper pronunciation of Greek and Latin, emphasized the desirability of learning things by heart, and refined the earlier list of selected reading. Here the recommended books were much more oriented toward governance, perhaps reflecting Vives's tacit acknowledgment that Mary was destined to rule. She was to read Cicero, Seneca, Plutarch, and the dialogues of Plato, "particularly those which demonstrate the government of the commonwealth," together with Thomas More's *Utopia* and Erasmus's *Institutio Principis Christiani*.

Vives's curriculum did allow for a few stories for Mary's amusement, but they were carefully selected and focused heavily on the deeds of self-sacrificing women. Mary could read about the virtuous Roman matron Lucretia, who, after being raped by the son of Tarquin the Proud, stabbed herself to death; or about the patient Griselda, whose husband put her through endless trials to assure himself of her devotion. These were stories that taught "the art of life" and that Mary could "tell to others."[4] As Mary got older, Vives advised that Katherine revise her educational program more precisely: "Time will admonish her as to more exact details, and thy singular wisdom will discover for her what they should be."[5]

GIVEN KATHERINE'S own intellect, much was anticipated of Mary. As Erasmus wrote to the queen in his *Christiani Matrimonii Institutio*, "Your qualities are known to us . . . we expect a work no less of your daughter Mary. For what should we not expect from a girl who is born of the most devout of parents and brought up under the care of such a mother?[6] Mary in fact proved to be a highly accomplished child. She was able to write a letter in Latin by the age of nine and at twelve translated the prayer of Saint Thomas Aquinas. Henry Parker, a literary noble, wrote in a later dedication to Mary, "I do well remember that scant you were twelve years of age but that you were so ripe in the Latin tongue, that rare doth happen to the woman sex, that your grace could not only perfectly read, write and construe Latin, but furthermore translate any hard thing of the Latin into our English tongue."[7]

But Mary would also receive an education for life and rule that went beyond the strictures of Vives's instruction. She proved to be precocious and talented and shared her father's love of music. When at the age of two she heard the Venetian organist Dionysius Memo playing at court, she ran after him calling "Priest, Priest" and refusing to stop until he agreed to play more.[8] By the age of four Mary was playing the virginals and would later win lavish praise for her lute playing. Like her parents, she liked to hawk and to hunt, and as a teenager she developed a love of gambling at cards: her privy purse accounts reveal numerous amounts lost in this way.[9] Mary developed her own style, loved fine clothes and jewelry, and, eager to please, would happily dance and perform at court as foreign ambassadors sued for her hand.

CHAPTER 6

GREAT SIGNS AND TOKENS OF LOVE

∴

*Matters have gone so far, that the Queen sent her Confessor to me
in secret to warn me of Henry's discontents. She is very sorry that
your Majesty [Charles V] ever promised so much in this treaty,
and she fears it may one day be the cause of a weakening of the
friendship between you two.*[1]

—LOUIS DE PRAET TO CHARLES V,
MARCH 26, 1524

IN THE SUMMER OF 1523, HENRY AND CHARLES EMBARKED ON THE
"Great Enterprise," the joint invasion of France that they had agreed
upon the year before. It proved to be a debacle. At the end of August,
an English force of around 11,000 troops began a march toward Paris
but was forced back by French resistance and severe weather. When
Charles failed to open an offensive in France as he had promised, the
Anglo-imperial alliance reached the breaking point. Mistrustful of his
ally's fidelity, Henry began to consider the prospect of dissolving the
marriage treaty with the emperor and began talks for a match between
Mary and his sister's son, the young Scottish king, James V.[2] By the
end of October it looked as if agreement were in sight. Wolsey sent
word to Margaret that Henry would "find the means" to break Mary's
engagement with Charles "in brief time" and then "conclude the marriage" between his daughter and "his dearest nephew, the young King
of Scots."[3]

But the old alliances soon regained their appeal. On the morning of
February 24, 1525, imperial troops decisively defeated the French army
outside the walls of the city of Pavia. The French king was captured in

battle and taken to Madrid in the custody of the emperor. Charles was in the ascendancy, and Henry now looked to revive the Anglo-imperial plans for the dismemberment of France.[4] "Now is the time," Henry declared to an ambassador from the Low Countries, "for the Emperor and myself to devise the means of getting full satisfaction from France. Not an hour is to be lost." Henry would receive the French Crown, which belonged to him "by just title of inheritance." In return he would hand Mary over to Charles when she came of age, without any guarantee as to "how she should be entreated and ordered touching her marriage."[5]

Katherine also began to petition Charles, appealing on the grounds of family loyalty. She lamented that she had heard nothing from him for a long time, choosing to attribute his silence to the "inconstancy and fickleness of the sea":

> Nothing indeed would be so painful to me as to think that your Highness had forgotten me, and therefore beg and entreat, as earnestly as I can, that your Highness be pleased to inform me of your health, and send me your orders, for love and consanguinity both demand that we should write to each other oftener.[6]

Katherine tried to reassure herself that "as long as our nephew keeps his promise to marry our daughter the alliance will remain unbroken; as long as the marriage treaty stands, he may be sure of England."[7]

IN APRIL, AT WOLSEY'S instigation, Mary sent Charles an emerald ring as a symbol of her "constancy." Accompanying it was a message that she sought "for a better knowledge to be had when God shall send them grace to be together, whether his Majesty doth keep constant and continent to her, as with God's grace she will." The envoys added that Mary's love for Charles was so passionate that it was confirmed by jealousy, "one of the great signs and tokens of love."[8]

Upon receiving the ring Charles put it on his little finger and ordered the ambassadors to say that he would wear it for the sake of the princess for the rest of his life.[9] Although his affection for Mary could not be doubted, Charles now looked to disavow her as his future bride. It was still five years before Mary could marry, and Charles was now in pursuit of another cousin, Isabella of Portugal, who was of marriageable age. He was anxious to be married at once so he could leave his new empress to rule Spain while he traveled to his other territories and sought to break off the English match by proposing unrealistic terms. He would raise an army for the invasion of France provided that Henry would pay for it and that Mary was handed over at once so that she might "learn the Castilian language and the manners of the people."[10] If Henry would not agree to his requests, Charles would demand to be released from the agreement.[11]

Henry refused, and Wolsey made his excuses. Mary would not be given up on account of "the tenderness of her age" and, given "the respect to be had to her noble person," it was "not meet as yet" that she "endure the pains of the sea, nor also to be brought up in an other air, that may be dangerous to her person." Henry agreed to break off the betrothal on condition that Charles made peace with France and pay his debts to England.[12] Within days the emperor signed a contract with Isabella of Portugal, whom he married in February of the following year.

The Anglo-Spanish alliance was at an end. To Katherine it was a personal affront, and she protested at her nephew's behavior: "I am sure I deserve not this treatment, for such are my affection and readiness for your Highness's service that I deserved a better reward."[13] For Mary, who had quickly become enamored of her Spanish cousin, it meant a painful rejection but the beginning of an attachment that would endure for the rest of her life.

CHAPTER 7

PRINCESS OF WALES

∴

ALTHOUGH MARY WAS COURTED BY THE RULING FAMILIES OF EUROPE, Henry remained reluctant to accept her as his successor and continued to hope for a male heir. But Katherine had not conceived since 1518. She was now forty and, as the Venetian ambassador observed, "past that age in which women most commonly were wont to be fruitful."[1] Rumors had circulated in Rome in 1514 that the "King of England meant to repudiate his present wife . . . because he is unable to have children by her."[2] Mary's birth had once given Henry reason to hope; now, with no prospect of an heir, he began to reflect on the consequences of his "childlessness."

On June 16, 1525, Henry's bastard son, Henry Fitzroy, the product of a brief affair with one of the queen's ladies, Elizabeth Blount, was recognized as the king's son and showered with titles and honors. He was installed as a Knight of the Garter and created earl of Nottingham, duke of Richmond, and duke of Somerset. This unprecedented double dukedom was then followed by his appointments as lord high admiral and warden general of the Scottish Marches and, two years later, by his investiture as lord lieutenant of Ireland. Not since the twelfth century had a king of England raised an illegitimate son to the peerage, and never had any subject held such a collection of offices and titles. Fitzroy was now given a great household and sent to Sheriff Hutton Castle in Yorkshire as the head of the King's Council of the North. Lorenzo Orio, the Venetian envoy, reported that "he is now next in rank to His Majesty, and might yet be easily by the King's means exalted to higher things."[3] Katherine was indignant and feared that Mary might be excluded outright from her inheritance. "No bastard," she complained, "ought to be exalted above the daughter of the Queen."[4]

But Henry had not yet resolved to prefer one child to another, and preparations were being made to enhance Mary's status. The nine-year-old was to be dispatched to the Welsh Marches, one of the most desolate and volatile areas of the kingdom, to preside over the Council of Wales and the Marches. While Henry stopped short of formally investing her with the title "princess of Wales" and thereby explicitly acknowledging her as his successor, Mary's appointment represented the revival of an association of the king's heir with the government of Wales that had begun under Edward, the firstborn son of Edward IV, and followed by Prince Arthur more than twenty years before.[5]

Though Katherine would mourn her daughter's absence, she would take comfort from the fact that the princess's status was at last being recognized.[6] She was now following the path of the heir to the throne.

ON AUGUST 12, 1525, Mary left Wolsey's manor, The More, near St. Albans, for the Marches, accompanied by a vast entourage dressed in her livery colors of blue and green. From Woburn, then to Reading, she reached Thornbury Castle in Gloucestershire on or about the twenty-fourth. Dozens of carts had been borrowed from local establishments to carry all the necessary household items and furnishings, ranging from "3 brass pots, one brazen pestle and mortar, a frying pan with a flesh hook and a chest with irons for keeping prisoners" to a throne for the Presence Chamber and all that was necessary to furnish the chapel at Thornbury, including standing candelabras, Mass books with golden covers, carved stands, kneeling cushions, and prayer stools.[7]

It was to be a court in miniature. Lord Ferrers and Lord Dudley headed the establishment as steward and chamberlain, respectively; Bishop John Voysey was appointed lord president of the Council, and Margaret Pole, the countess of Salisbury, who had been dismissed from Mary's service in 1521 when her son the duke of Buckingham had been executed for treason, was reappointed lady mistress. Beneath these head officers were three hundred other servants, including Mary's new schoolmaster, Richard Fetherstone.[8]

The king's instructions detailed precisely the expectations and duties of the household and Council and made provision for Mary's education, welfare, and pastimes. The main responsibility was placed with Margaret Pole, who was entrusted with "all such things as concern the person of the said princess, her noble education and training in all virtuous demeanour." Mary was to be treated as "so great a princess doth appertain." Ladies and gentlewomen were to remain in attendance of her and were to "use themselves sadly, honourably, virtuously and discreetly in words, countenance, gesture, behaviour and deed with humility, reverence, lowliness . . . so as of them proceed no manner of example of evil or unfitting manner or conditions, but rather all good and godly behaviour." She was to learn to serve God, to take "moderate exercise" in the "open air," in gardens, sweet and wholesome places, so as to "confer unto her health, solace and comfort" as her lady governess thought "most convenient." At some seasons she was to pass her time

at her virginals, or other instruments musical, so that the same be not too much, and without fatigacion or weariness to intend to her learning of Latin tongue or French. At other seasons to dance, and amongst the residue to have good respect unto her diet, which is mete to be pure, well-prepared, dressed and served, with comfortable, joyous and merry communication in all honourable and virtuous manner.

Her clothes, her chamber, and her body were to be kept "pure, sweet, clean and wholesome."[9]

With mother and daughter now apart, they maintained a correspondence, and Katherine resolved to remain closely involved in Mary's education, writing her:

Daughter,
I pray you think not that any forgetfulness hath caused me to
keep Charles [her messenger] so long here, and answered not to your
good Letter . . . the long absence of the King and you troubleth me.
My health is meetly good: and I trust in God, he that sent me the
last doth it to the best, and will shortly turn it to the first to come to

good effect. And in the meantime I am very glad to hear from You, specially when they show me that you be well amended. I pray God to continue it to his pleasure. As for your writing in Latin I am glad that you shall change from me to Master Fetherstone, for that shall do you much good, to learn by him to write right. But yet sometimes I would be glad when you do write to Master Fetherstone of your own editing when he hath read it that I may see it. For it shall be a great comfort to me to see You keep your Latin and fair writing and all. And so I pray You to recommend me to my Lady of Salisbury. At Woburn this Friday night,

Your loving mother,
Katherine the Queen.[10]

MARY'S HOUSEHOLD WOULD become the center of a social elite and of high courtly culture. Full royal ceremony was observed, with Mary practicing the part of queen at the head of her own court. Every day at least "two Gentleman Ushers, two Gentleman Waiters, two Yeoman Ushers, twelve Yeomen and two Grooms" were to attend her in the Presence Chamber, and more were to be added on "Sundays, Saturdays and other principal seasons," when there "shall be access or recourse of noblemen or other strangers repairing unto that court or that it be as festival days or times or other things requisite to have be great and honourable presence."[11]

Such numbers were expected to flock to Tewkesbury to pay homage to the princess that John Voysey, the bishop of Exeter and lord president of the Council, anxiously wrote to Wolsey asking, on account of the "great repair of strangers" anticipated, that "a ship of silver for the almes dish" be sent to hold the princess's napkin, which afterward would be filled with scraps to be distributed among the poor. Voysey also inquired what provision would be made for the Twelfth Night banquet entertainments and whether they should employ a "Lord of Misrule," and requested that trumpets and a rebeck (a type of fiddle) be sent to Thornbury.[12]

At the center of her own court, Mary began to learn the art of governance. Her French tutor, Giles Duwes, later wrote *An Introductory for to Learn to Read, to Pronouce, and to Speak French* based on his time in the household in the Marches. In it he portrayed Mary as a princely ruler and her court as a center of literary patronage, educated conversation, and gentle manners. Mary features in a number of dialogues about piety, philosophy, and courtly love. In one, Duwes recalled an occasion when the young princess participated in the drawing of names on Valentine's Day. When Mary drew as her valentine her treasurer, Sir Ralph Egerton—an old man afflicted by gout—she insisted on calling him her "husband *adoptif.*" As his pretend wife, she criticized Sir Ralph for taking better care of his gout "than you do your wife." She could hardly believe "that the gout might withhold a good husband having some love to his wife" and begged him to teach her what "a good husband ought to teach his wife," that is, the definition of love.[13] She had just turned ten.

CHAPTER 8

PEARL OF THE WORLD

∴

EVER SINCE CHARLES V HAD BROKEN OFF HIS BETROTHAL TO MARY, Wolsey had been in negotiations to revive an alliance with France. In March 1526, Francis had reentered his kingdom, having been in imperial captivity since the Battle of Pavia the previous year. By the terms of the Treaty of Madrid, which had secured Francis his freedom from imperial custody, he had handed over his two sons as hostages for the payment of his ransom and was contracted to marry Eleanor, the widowed queen of Portugal.

But Francis had no intention of keeping to these terms. As soon as possible, he told the English ambassadors, "I shall take off my mask."[1] Now seeking revenge, he joined a league formed at Cognac that comprised the pope, Venice, Milan, and Florence and looked to force the victorious imperial armies out of Italy. Wolsey, always hoping to enhance England's status by acting as the "peacemaker of Europe," sought an Anglo-French entente to compel Charles to moderate his settlement with Francis and prevent further war. Mary was once again to be used as a gambit for an alliance. As she was quickly learning, marriage was for political, not personal, ends. Mutual and sacred vows were made and unmade as the balance of power between England, France, and Spain dictated. As Nicholas von Schomberg, archbishop of Capua, wrote to the emperor, "in time of war the English make use of the princess as an owl, with which to lure birds."[2]

❧

IN JULY, JOHN CLERK, bishop of Bath and Wells, was sent to France with instructions to renew marriage negotiations for a match between Mary and Francis's second son, Henry, duke of Orléans. Mary was, Clerk declared, "the pearl of the world" and "the jewel that his highness [Henry VIII] esteemed more than anything in earth."[3] As the negotiations proceeded, Henry intervened with a proposal that he give up his ancient claim to France and join the League of Cognac, provided that Francis pay him a pension, cede Boulogne, and marry Mary himself.[4] Francis, recently widowed, was only two years younger than Henry and a notorious womanizer. Yet for English interests the alliance made good sense. If Francis predeceased Henry and left children by Mary, the English and French succession would remain separate, as Francis already had two sons. If Henry died first, Francis could claim England through his wife. But his reign was likely to be short, given his age, and then the two kingdoms would become separate once more. At first Francis was skeptical of Henry's plan, but after the pope declared the match a *sancta conjunctio*—a holy union—Francis responded favorably to the proposal, seeing it as a valuable alliance against imperial designs.

The French king now proceeded to praise Mary's abilities, concluding that given "her education, her form and fashion, her beauty and virtue, and what father and mother she cometh of; expedient and necessary it shall be for me and for my realm that I marry her." He reassured the English ambassador, "I have as great a mind to her as ever I had to any woman."[5] Francis wrote to Mary, addressing her as "high and powerful princess" and assuring her of his loyalty as her good brother, cousin, and ally.[6] In February 1527, a legation left France for England to conclude the terms of an alliance.

ON APRIL 23, as the court celebrated the Feast of Saint George at Greenwich, Mary received the French visitors. She spoke to them in Latin, French, and Italian and entertained them on the virginals.[7] The principal French ambassador, the marquess of Turenne, declared that he was impressed by her accomplishments but observed that she was "so thin, spare and small as to make it impossible for her to be married for the next three years."[8] Francis's mother, Louise of Savoy, the queen regent, proposed that the marriage should take place at Calais in August, and after the solemnization, the king, her son, might "abide

Huggard, W. J. "Katherine Parr: Religious Convictions of a Renaissance Queen," *Renaissance Quarterly* 22 (1969), pp. 346–59.

Hughes, Philip. *The Reformation in England*, 3 vols. (London, 1950–54).

Hume, M. A. S. *Two English Queens, and Philip* (London, 1908).

Hunt, A. *The Drama of Coronation: Medieval Ceremony in Early Modern England* (Cambridge, 2008).

Ives, E. W. *Anne Boleyn* (Oxford, 1989).

———. "Henry VIII's Will: A Forensic Conundrum," *The Historical Journal* 35, no. 4 (December 1992), pp. 779–804.

———. "Henry VIII's Will: The Protectorate Provisions of 1546–7," *The Historical Journal* 37, no. 4 (1994), pp. 901–14.

James, M. E. "Obedience and Dissent in Henrican England: The Lincolnshire Rebellion of 1536," *Past and Present* 48 (1970), pp. 3–78.

James, S. E. *Kathryn Parr, the Making of a Queen* (Aldershot, 1999).

Jansen, S. L. *The Monstrous Regiment of Women: Female Rulers in Early Modern Europe* (Basingstoke, 2002).

Jones, M. K., and M. G. Underwood. *The King's Mother: Lady Margaret Beaufort Countess of Richmond and Derby* (Cambridge, 1992).

Jordan, W. K. *Edward VI: The Threshold of Power* (London, 1970).

———. *Edward VI: The Young King. The Protectorship of the Duke of Somerset* (London, 1968).

Kamen, Henry. *Philip of Spain* (New Haven, 1997).

Kelly, H. A. *The Matrimonial Trials of Henry VIII* (Stanford, Calif., 1976).

Levin, C., et al., eds. *"High and Mighty Queens" of Early Modern England: Realities and Representations* (New York, 2003).

Levine, M. *Tudor Dynastic Problems, 1460–1571* (London, 1973).

Loach, J. *Edward VI* (London, 1999).

———. "The Function of Ceremonial in the Reign of Henry VIII," *Past and Present* 142 (1994), pp. 43–68.

———. "The Marian Establishment and the Printing Press," *English Historical Review* 100 (1986), pp. 135–48.

———. "Mary Tudor and the Re-Catholicisation of England," *History Today* 44, no. 1 (1994), pp. 16–22.

———. "Pamphlets and Politics, 1553–8," *Bulletin of the Institute of Historical Research* 48 (1975), pp. 31–45.

———. *Parliament and the Crown in the Reign of Mary Tudor* (Oxford, 1986).

Loach, J., and Tittler, R., eds. *The Mid-Tudor Polity, c. 1540–60* (Basingstoke, 1983).

Loades, D. M. "The Enforcement of Reaction, 1553–8," *Journal of Ecclesiastical History* 16 (1965), pp. 54–66.

———. *John Dudley, Duke of Northumberland* (Oxford, 1996).

———. *Mary Tudor: A Life* (Oxford, 1989).

———. *Mary Tudor: The Tragical History of the First Queen of England* (Kew, 2006).

———. *The Oxford Martyrs* (London, 1970).

———. "Philip II and the Government of England," in *Law and Government under the Tudors: Essays Presented to Sir Geoffrey Elton*, ed. C. Cross, D. M. Loades, and J. J. Scarisbrick (Cambridge, 1988), pp. 177–94.

———. "The Reign of Mary Tudor: Historiography and Research," *Albion* 21, no. 4 (1989), pp. 547–58.

———. *The Reign of Mary Tudor: Politics, Government and Religion in England 1553–59*, 2nd ed. (London, 1991).

———. *Two Tudor Conspiracies* (Cambridge, 1965).

Loades, D. M., ed. *John Foxe: An Historical Perspective* (Aldershot, 1990).

MacCulloch, D. "Kett's Rebellion in Context," *Past and Present* 84 (1979), pp. 36–59.

———. "Kett's Rebellion in Context: A Rejoinder," *Past and Present* 93 (1981), pp. 165–73.

———. *Thomas Cranmer, A Life* (London, 1996).

———. *Tudor Church Militant, Edward VI and the Protestant Reformation* (London, 1999).

Maltby, William S. *The Black Legend in England: The Development of Anti-Spanish Sentiment, 1558–1660* (Durham, N.C., 1971).

———. *The Reign of Charles V* (Basingstoke, 2002).

Manning, Revd. C. R. "State Papers Relating to the Custody of the Princess Elizabeth at Woodstock in 1554," *Norfolk Archaeology* 4 (1855), pp. 133–226.

Mattingly, Garrett. *Catherine of Aragon* (London, 1942).

Mayer, Thomas F. *Reginald Pole, Prince and Prophet* (Cambridge, 2000).

Mcintosh, J. L. *From Heads of Household to Heads of State: The Preaccession Households of Mary and Elizabeth Tudor, 1516–1558* (Columbia University Press, 2008).

Medvei, V. C. "The Illness and Death of Mary Tudor," *Journal of the Royal Society of Medicine* 80 (1987), pp. 766–70.

Miller, H. "Henry VIII's Unwritten Will: Grants of Lands and Honours in 1547," in *Wealth and Power in Tudor England: Essays Presented to S. T. Bindoff*, ed. E. W. Ives, R. J. Knecht, and J. J. Scarisbrick (London, 1978), pp. 87–105.

Moore, D. "Recorder Fleetwood and the Tudor Queenship Controversy," in *Ambiguous Realities: Women in the Middle Ages and Renaissance*, ed. Carole Levin and Jeanie Watson (Detroit, 1987), pp. 235–51.

Muller, J. A. *Stephen Gardiner and the Tudor Reaction* (London, 1926).

Parker, Geoffrey. *Philip II* (Chicago, 1995).

Paul, J. E. *Catherine of Aragon and Her Friends* (London, 1966).

Pierce, Hazel. *Margaret Pole, 1473–1541* (Cardiff, 2003).

Pogson, Rex H. "Reginald Pole and the Priorities of Government in Mary Tudor's Church," *Historical Journal* 18 (1975), pp. 3–21.

———. "Revival and Reform in Mary Tudor's Church," *Journal of Ecclesiastical History* 25 (1974), pp. 249–65.

Pollard, A. F. *The History of England from the Accession of Edward VI to the Death of Elizabeth* (London, 1913).

Prescott, H. F. M. *Mary Tudor* (London, 1940).

Redworth, G. *In Defence of the Church Catholic: The Life of Stephen Gardiner* (Oxford, 1990).

———. "Matters Impertinent to Women: Male and Female Monarchy under Philip and Mary," *English Historical Review* 112, no. 447 (June 1999), pp. 597–613.

Richards, J. M. *Mary Tudor* (Basingstoke, 2008).

———. "Mary Tudor as 'Sole Quene'? Gendering Tudor Monarchy," *Historical Journal* 40 (1997), pp. 895–99.

———. "To Promote a Woman to Beare Rule," *The Sixteenth Century Journal* 28, no. 1 (1997), pp. 101–21.

Robinson, W. R. B. "Princess Mary's Itinerary in the Marches of Wales, 1525–1527: A Provisional Record," *Historical Research* 71 (1998), pp. 233–52.

Rodriguez-Salgado, M. J. *The Changing Face of Empire: Charles V, Philip II and Habsburg Authority, 1551–1559* (Cambridge, 1988).

Russell, E. "Mary Tudor and Mr Jorkins," *Historical Research* 63, no. 152 (1990), pp. 263–76.

Russell, J. G. *The Field of the Cloth of Gold* (London, 1969).

Samman, N. "The Progresses of Henry VIII, 1509–1529," in *The Reign of Henry VIII: Politics, Policy and Piety*, ed. D. MacCulloch (Basingstoke, 1995), pp. 59–74.

Samson, Alexander. "Changing Places: The Marriage and Royal Entry of Philip, Prince of Austria and Mary Tudor, July–August 1554," *The Sixteenth Century Journal* 36, no. 3 (2005), pp. 761–84.

Scarisbrick, J. J. *Henry VIII* (London, 1968).

Schenk, W. *Reginald Pole, Cardinal of England* (London, 1950).

Sherlock, Peter. "The Monuments of Elizabeth Tudor and Mary Stuart: King James and the Manipulation of Memory," *Journal of British Studies* 46 (April 2007), pp. 263–89.

Skidmore, Chris. *Edward VI: The Lost King of England* (London, 2007).

Starkey, David. *Elizabeth: Apprenticeship* (London, 2001).

————. *Henry VIII: A European Court in England* (London, 1991).

————. *Six Wives: The Queens of Henry VIII* (London, 2004).

Stone, J. M. *The History of Mary I, Queen of England* (London, 1901).

Strickland, A. *Lives of the Queens of England,* 6 vols. (London, 1854).

Thorp, M. R. "Religion and the Wyatt Rebellion of 1554," *Church History* 47 (1978), pp. 363–80.

Thurley, S. *The Royal Palaces of Tudor England: Architecture and Court Life, 1460–1547* (London, 1993).

Tittler, R., and S. Battley. "The Local Community and the Crown in 1553: The Accession of Mary Tudor Revisited," *Bulletin of the Institute of Historical Research* 57 (1984), pp. 131–39.

Waldman, M. *The Lady Mary* (London, 1972).

Walker, Julia. "Reading the Tombs of Elizabeth I," *English Literary Renaissance* 26, no. 3 (1996), pp. 510–30.

Watson, F., ed. *Vives and the Renascence Education of Women* (London, 1912).

Weikel, A. "The Marian Council Re-visited," in *The Mid-Tudor Polity, 1540–1560,* ed. J. Loach and R. Tittler (London, 1980).

————. "The Rise and Fall of a Marian Privy Councillor: Sir Henry Bedingfield 1509/11–1585," in *Norfolk Archaeology* 40 (1987), pp. 73–83.

Whitelock, A. "A Woman in a Man's World: Mary I and Political Intimacy, 1553–1558," *Women's History Review* 16, no. 3 (2007), pp. 323–34.

Whitelock, A., and D. MacCulloch. "Princess Mary's Household and the Succession Crisis, July 1553," *The Historical Journal* 50, no. 2 (2007), pp. 265–87.

Wiesener, Louis. *La Jeunesse d'Elisabeth d'Angleterre, 1533–1558* (Paris, 1878).

Williams, P. *The Council in the Marches of Wales under Elizabeth I* (Cardiff, 1958).

Withington, Robert. *English Pageantry: An Historical Outline,* 2 vols. (Cambridge, 1918).

Wizeman, William. *The Theology and Spirituality of Mary Tudor's Church* (Aldershot, 2006).

Wooding, Lucy E. C. *Rethinking Catholicism in Marian England* (Oxford, 2000).

INDEX